The *Grand* American Home

The Grand American Home

WESKetch Architecture

images
Publishing

Published in Australia in 2008 by
The Images Publishing Group Pty Ltd
ABN 89 059 734 431
6 Bastow Place, Mulgrave, Victoria 3170, Australia
Tel: +61 3 9561 5544 Fax: +61 3 9561 4860
books@imagespublishing.com
www.imagespublishing.com

Copyright © The Images Publishing Group Pty Ltd 2008
The Images Publishing Group Reference Number: 742

National Library of Australia Cataloguing-in-Publication entry:

Kaufman, William E.S.
The Grand American Home WESKetch Architecture.

1st ed.

Bibliography.

ISBN 9781864701814 (hbk.).

1. WESKetch Architecture (Firm). 2. Architectural firms – United States.

3. Architecture, Domestic – United States. I. Title.

720.973

Coordinating editor; Janelle McCulloch

Designed by The Graphic Image Studio Pty Ltd, Mulgrave, Australia
www.tgis.com.au

Digital production by Splitting Image Colour Studio Pty Ltd, Australia

Printed by Paramount Printing Company Limited Hong Kong

IMAGES has included on its website a page for special notices in relation to this and our other publications. Please visit www.imagespublishing.com.

Contents

Preface

Americans have long been obsessed with their houses. The quest to stake one's claim on a piece of land, build a home, raise a family, and leave behind a legacy is, after all, "The Great American Dream." This book contains a number of translations of these dreams, which fuse the inspirational ideas of our clients with the many talents of the architects within WESKetch Architecture, Inc. The homes depicted are truly American, and offer a proverbial melting pot of ideas, as well as cultural and contextual amalgamations. They do not represent any particular style or period but rather are vernacular in the sense that they belong to their environments while at times referencing the treasured craft and texture of a forgotten past.

Architecture and the art of traditional building and place-making has evolved over time, through a process of applied craftsmanship. But it has also been a need born out of necessity. All homes are built out of some necessity, either perceived or real. And because of this, a home is by far the most difficult of all places to design well. It is both a place of private contemplation and one of public display. It is a place to cook and a place to eat; a place to serve and a place to be served; essentially, it's a place to *live*. WESKetch's goal is to craft our homes with common threads of honesty, passion, patience, and skill, as well as create places that inspire life, and embrace the notion of being alive.

Creating an invigorating sense of place that is sustainable over many generations is a rewarding process. Effective communication of any language—written, spoken, or constructed—is truly an art. Our learned ability to translate the functional and aesthetic requirements of our clients into timeless buildings and do it in a fresh new way each time is the staple of our craft.

I was raised and trained in the tradition of the master craftsman; mentored and apprenticed in a fashion that taught me to respect the beauty and endurance of the past. Through WESKetch Architecture, we preserve and protect the character of place through the creation of sustainable, timeless structures, while maintaining the detailed qualities seemingly lost in contemporary buildings.

The success of WESKetch Architecture stems from this determination to connect with the past while at the same time looking forward, in a visionary manner. The principles that drive the creative forces of the firm are generated not only from an appreciation for tradition, but also from deep within the individual roots of the organization. Unlike many art forms, architecture is truly a collaborative effort. Alliances of diverse but talented teams, including architects of all skill levels and experiences, interior designers, master craftsmen, and landscape professionals, help to execute the result, sometimes in spectacular fashion.

Nestled in a picturesque country village in the central New Jersey landscape, WESKetch Architecture is becoming renowned for offering a fountain of ideas and innovations that truly stand the test of time. In an era where it seems almost fashionable to find disingenuous solutions to legitimate design problems, WESKetch Architecture has succeeded in creating classic, timeless homes while answering all the requirements of modern living.

The designs featured in this book are an eclectic selection of individual styles, materials, and forms. But what all of these homes have in common is a harmonious combination of programmatic and aesthetic sensibilities embedded in the regional vernacular of their respective surroundings. Each home is graced with meticulous attention to detail and combines high technology with healthy building environments. The results are a unique blend of modern lifestyles and articulately crafted traditional constructions. The past meeting the future in the present.

William E.S. Kaufman

Foreword

During the past 20 years, American domestic architecture has undergone a revival of sorts. Following the waning of postmodernism, and continuing their critique of the sterile, grim formalism of modernist domestic architecture, American architects have begun the process of embracing and re-learning the classical canon and re-connecting with a tradition of domestic design that has developed over a period of almost 300 years in the New World. Spurred by a new generation of smart, affluent, and demanding clients, architects throughout the United States have been producing convincing, beautiful, and innovative traditional houses that combine the best of the American vernacular with the latest in domestic technologies. Moreover, many of these purportedly "nostalgic" or "historical" buildings have also been at the cutting edge of environmental sustainability, employing traditional, recyclable materials that are friendly to the earth in more than superficial ways.

On the Eastern Seaboard of the U.S., a new school of traditionalists has emerged, largely under the influence of teacher/practitioners such as Allan Greenberg, Robert Stern, and Thomas Gordon Smith. These architects defy classification. Their organizational allegiances are loose; many would consider themselves "New Urbanists," and a large number have joined New York's Institute of Classical Architecture and Classical America. But others see themselves as free from labels or schools. William E.S. Kaufman is such an architect. His firm, WESKetch Architecture, has carved a unique path for itself since its formation in the mid-1990s.

As the first LEED-acredited architect in New Jersey, Mr. Kaufman has long identified himself with sustainable design and environmental causes. Unlike many architects with such credentials, he has refused to associate sustainability with modernist design or technology, maintaining a diverse practice that builds with reverence for the past. Educated at the New Jersey Institute of Technology, Kaufman has worked in both commercial and residential arenas since the 1980s. When he began his practice, he vowed to connect his work with a craft tradition that he learned in the construction trades. This, he says, led him away from a strictly modernist approach to design and toward one based upon a respect for traditions in building. He also found inspiration in the work of some of the English and American designers, such as Lutyens, Voysey, Richardson, and McKim, Mead & White, who continue to offer lessons to traditionalists today.

WESKetch Architecture has designed lively additions to historic houses by George B. Post and Henry Hardenburgh in the Somerset Hills of New Jersey, while also creating new houses with the charm and ambience of the early country houses in the area. The firm's commitment to sustainability is seen in a wonderful "retrofit" of a historic barn from western Pennsylvania, moved to a site in New Jersey. Much of the work has a refreshing, rustic spirit, reminding residents of central New Jersey of the horse farms, country estates, and villages that still give identity to the region today. The best designs from the firm, such as the charming "Cottage" on a large estate in the manner of a French dwelling, and the simple but artful "Crosspond Farm," betray a vigorous commitment to building with a sense of place and craft that is rare in contemporary architecture. "Knollwood," a playful take-off on the American Shingle Style, shows Kaufman's often whimsical sense of form to its best advantage. Clients have responded enthusiastically to WESKetch Architecture's approach to design—the firm has grown into a regional leader in not only residential but also multi-family, resort, and commercial architecture.

In short, Bill Kaufman has shown that architecture today can embrace tradition without sacrificing function, energy conservation, comfort, or craftsmanship. WESKetch Architecture will continue to pursue beautiful, place-specific, sustainable, and regionally appropriate solutions to the challenges architects face in designing for a changing American environment.

Mark A. Hewitt, AIA

Homes

1

Appletrees

Originally constructed in 1896 by the renowned architect George Post, this Neo-Classical estate had scarcely survived a hundred years of neglect before being heroically rescued by a prominent business executive and given a new lease of life. Once finished, it proved a perfect wedding gift for a well-to-do family.

The project underwent two major phases. The first was a restoration and renovation of the main residence. The second included various additions of numerous indoor and outdoor spaces to accommodate busy modern lifestyles.

The original home was garnished with covered porches and balconies, a feature common in Post's work. The first task was to expand the kitchen area by constructing a glass-roofed solarium immediately adjacent to the newly remodeled cooking space. This space provides for both informal family gatherings and small-scale entertaining. The room opens directly to a stone terrace covered with a natural cedar trellis by means of three 8-foot-high timber French doors. These doors were constructed using the most advanced structural glazing in order to achieve the maximum glass area.

In addition, a stable-style carriage house was designed to house six vehicles. This component was carefully detailed to create the illusion and scale of a historic carriage house. The scale of the automobile was practically erased with the installation of stable-style barn doors and antique market lighting. The placement of this structure encloses the stone tower and reflecting pool.

2

1   Front elevation
2   Approach

3

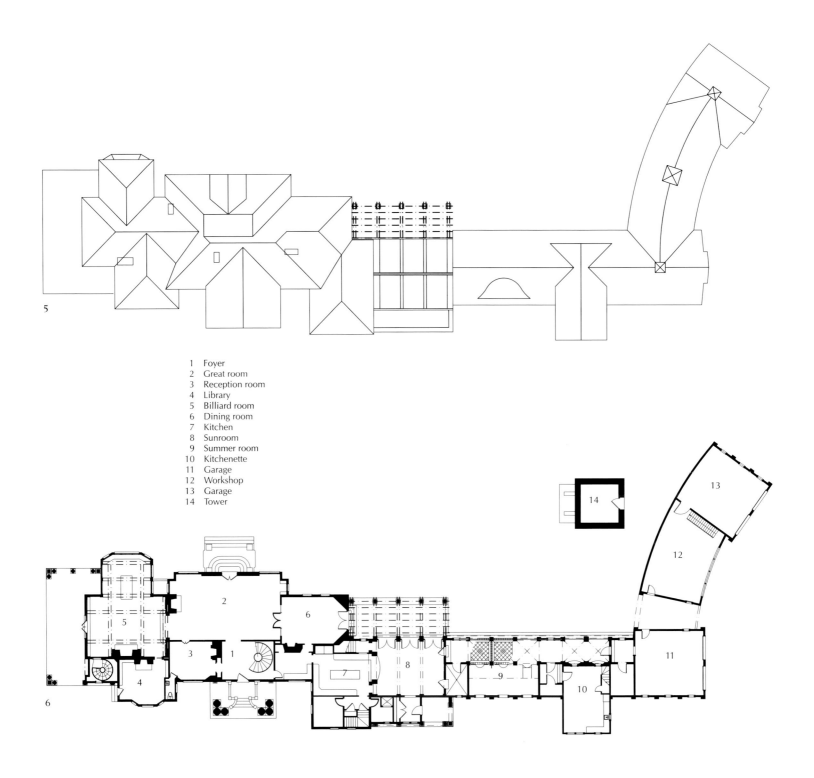

1 Foyer
2 Great room
3 Reception room
4 Library
5 Billiard room
6 Dining room
7 Kitchen
8 Sunroom
9 Summer room
10 Kitchenette
11 Garage
12 Workshop
13 Garage
14 Tower

5

6

7

9

10   Veranda
Opposite   Pergola at rear of sunroom

10

13

1

Beechwood

Inspired by the Shingle Style estates of such architectural luminaries as McKim, Mead & White, Lamb & Rich, and Bernard Maybeck, this rambling home was designed to satisfy its owners' desire for estate living and gracious rooms for entertaining while maintaining the informality and flow found in smaller homes. Early design cues were taken from the site, with the southern exposure and topography dictating the location of the house. The design also had to ensure that views were maximized and site disturbance minimized.

The cedar shingles and fieldstone of the exterior reinforce the home's harmony with the site, while the intersecting geometries of the plan help establish powerful axes throughout the house and maximize light and cross ventilation for virtually every room. The home's rambling footprint provides an element of constant discovery to the observer, and ensures that its overall size is never readily apparent, while creating myriad outdoor spaces that both embrace the landscape and seamlessly integrate with the interior.

The potential environmental impact of a residence of this nature was not ignored by either the owner or the architect. Many steps were taken to minimize that impact, ranging from a geothermal heating and cooling system to the highest performance windows and insulation available today. All materials specified were naturally regenerative and long-lasting. The environmental sustainability of the residence combined with the timeless appeal of the Shingle Style ensure that this house will retain its beauty for generations to come.

2

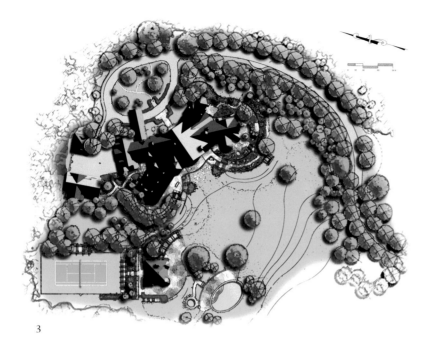

3

3 Site and landscape plan
4 Porte-cochère
5 Front entrance
6 Exterior façade details at study

4

5

7

8

9

10

11

7   Corner dormer
8   Eyebrow dormer
9   Cupola and chimneys
10   Archway to breakfast room
11   Bay dormer at rear entry

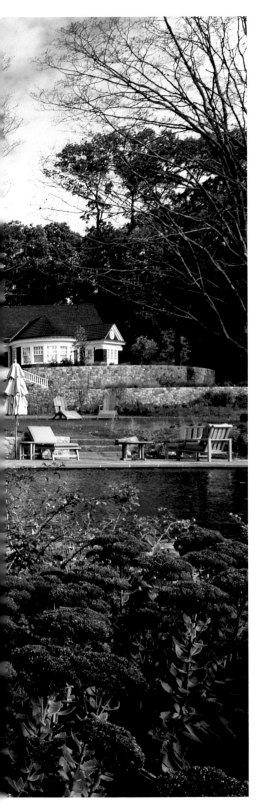

13

12 View from pool gardens
13 Cantilevered corner dormer
14 Pool house

14

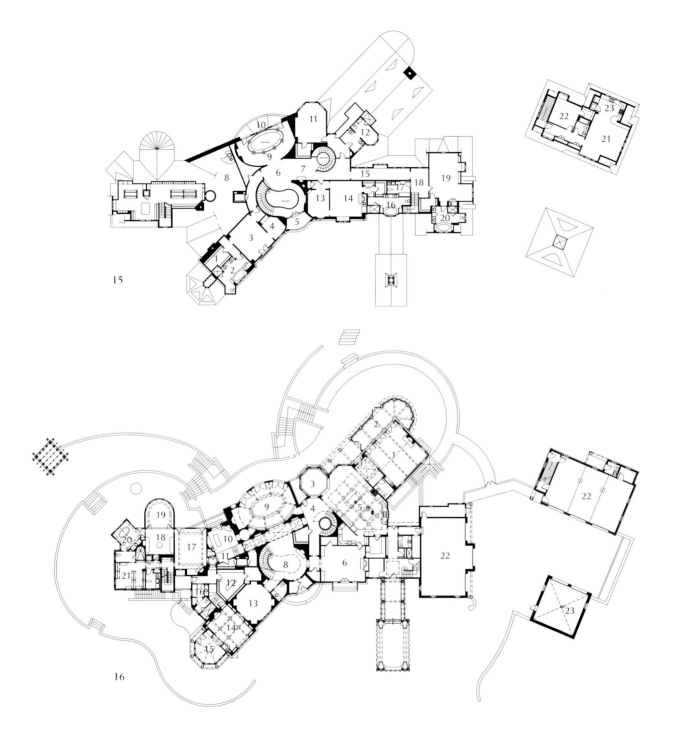

1 Closet
2 Bathroom
3 Bedroom
4 Sitting
5 Front balcony
6 Upper balcony
7 Hall
8 Unfinished attic
9 Great room balcony
10 Outdoor balcony
11 Bedroom
12 Bathroom
13 Sitting room
14 Bedroom
15 Hall
16 Bathroom
17 Laundry
18 Hall
19 Bedroom
20 Bathroom
21 Guest house living room
22 Guest house bedroom
23 Guest house kitchen

1 Family room
2 Rear porch
3 Breakfast room
4 Stair hall
5 Kitchen
6 Dining room
7 Entry
8 Foyer
9 Great room
10 Pub room
11 Hall
12 Master closet
13 Display
14 Library
15 Study
16 Master bathroom
17 Master bedroom
18 Dressing room
19 Sitting room
20 Master bathroom 2
21 Master closet 2
22 Garage
23 Garage

17

18

15 Second level plan
16 Ground level plan
17 Oval great room
18 Upper art gallery

19 Back stair with iron railing
20 Foyer
21 Brick wine cellar
22 Rear elevation
23 View from south

20

19

21

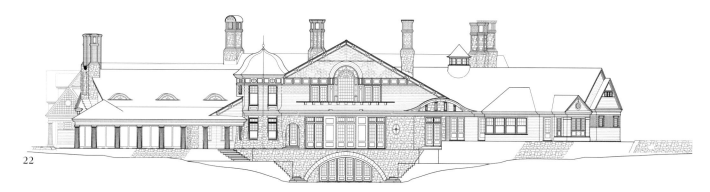

22

23

1

Bridle Paths

Based on what the Ancient Greeks referred to as a "sun trap," the complex plan of intersecting axes and grids at Bridle Paths allows most of the primary rooms to have windows on three walls. The English Tudor form, inspired by the owner, was adapted to form a classically modern building, so that the front of the home is constructed around an outer radius concentric to the circular motor court, inviting one into the home. The rear of the residence, meanwhile, splays outward, directly responsive to the polar axis and distant views of the hills beyond.

One enters Bridle Paths through a solid antique door into an open foyer, which acts as the focal center, organizer, and signature room of the house. There, in the style of a center hall, a parlor is located directly to the right and a formal dining room to the left. Directly opposite the front doors and adjacent to the main foyer is a large raised stone terrace with an outdoor fireplace that is oriented perfectly toward the distant views of the mountain range. The north wing is a renovated carriage house that has been converted to garages, a billiard room, and guest quarters.

Sprawling yards created by the dynamic plan provide an intimate and pleasantly scaled environment not typically associated with a house of this size. Solar orientation, views, prevailing winds, and vehicular access all played a vital role in the formation of this dynamic plan.

3 Upper level plan
4 Ground level plan
5 Garden folly
6 Window detail
7 Outdoor room
8 Roof detail
9 Veranda

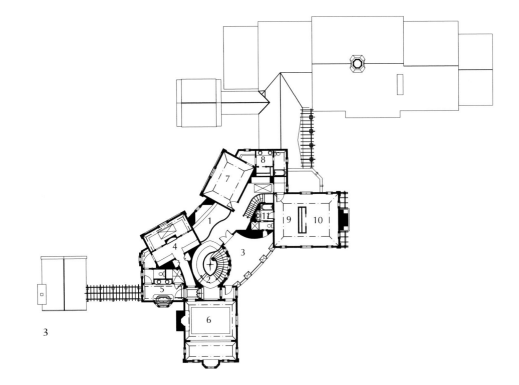

1 Upper foyer
2 Main stair
3 Balcony
4 Dressing room
5 Master bathroom
6 Master bedroom
7 Bedroom
8 Bathroom
9 Sitting area
10 Bedroom
11 Bathroom

3

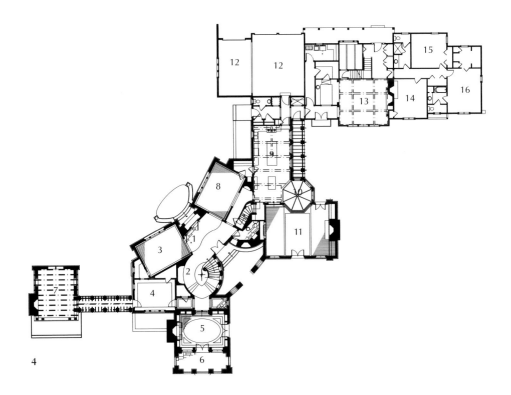

1 Foyer
2 Main stair
3 Living room
4 Den
5 Library
6 Balcony
7 Folly
8 Dining room
9 Kitchen
10 Breakfast room
11 Family room
12 Garage
13 Billiards
14 Bedroom
15 Bedroom
16 Bedroom

4

5

6

7

8

9

11

12

10　Billiard room
11　Family room
12　Library

13

14

Clarence Manor

Set amid a terrain of rocks and woods, this home is a powerful testament to classic design. The design is a modified version of the Greek sun trap or butterfly plan. Carved into the landscape to follow the natural topography of the site, the residence features a flowing floor plan to suit the needs of a growing family.

A grand, three-story circular tower stair provides an anchor for the public spaces and links the geometries of the architectural masses, providing a stunning backdrop upon which to greet visitors. The spiral "S" was fashioned particularly for the residence's owner, whose first name begins with that letter.

A uniquely designed garage was created as split carriage houses, allowing a seamless transition with the rest of the home. The porte-cochère between the garages separates public from private areas while providing a covered pathway to the home from the guest cottage.

The receiving courtyard is embraced by the enveloping architectural character of the façade—the axial focus being on the stone tower topped with crenellations. This inspiring space proves gaze-worthy at any time of day or night.

3

4

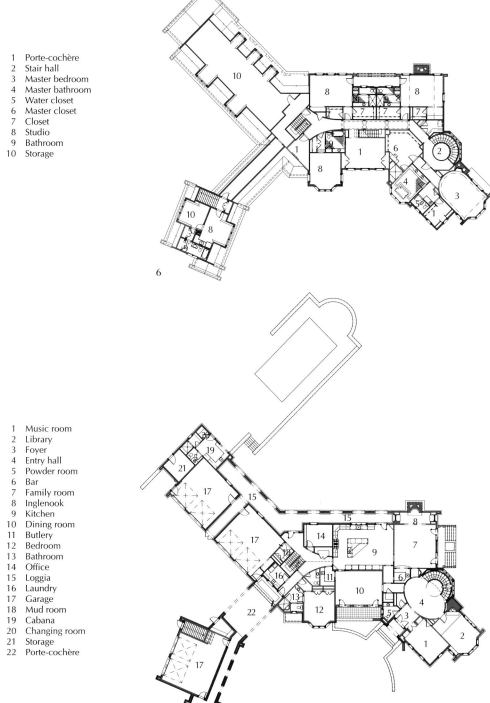

1 Porte-cochère
2 Stair hall
3 Master bedroom
4 Master bathroom
5 Water closet
6 Master closet
7 Closet
8 Studio
9 Bathroom
10 Storage

6

6 Upper level plan
7 Ground level plan
8 Entry
9 Dormer detail
10 Hardware
11 Gable detail

1 Music room
2 Library
3 Foyer
4 Entry hall
5 Powder room
6 Bar
7 Family room
8 Inglenook
9 Kitchen
10 Dining room
11 Butlery
12 Bedroom
13 Bathroom
14 Office
15 Loggia
16 Laundry
17 Garage
18 Mud room
19 Cabana
20 Changing room
21 Storage
22 Porte-cochère

7

8

9

10

11

13

14

15

16

12   Main stair
13   Stair detail
14   Kitchen
15   Fireplace
16   Inglenook

17

18

19

17 Upper tower
18 Bathroom
19 Shower detail

20

20 East garden
21 Carriage house
22 Pool

21

22

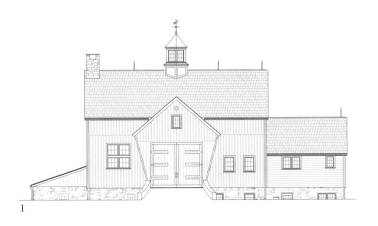

1

Coffeetown Barn

This old barn, originally built as a haybarn in western Pennsylvania in the 1840s, was located in Coffeetown, Pennsylvania; disassembled; placed in a warehouse; and rebuilt as a home on a 40-acre horse farm in Somerset County. The original structure's timber-frame was salvaged and re-erected and the rich, heavy timber detailing is now elegantly juxtaposed with the new finely crafted cabinetry, with the new rooms further united by an eclectic collection of fine furnishings.

Preserving the original beams and timbers of the old barn while adapting the spaces to the contemporary needs of the clients proved challenging. The result is a unique residence that combines all the modern luxuries and amenities of the 21st century within the rustic backdrop of the original barn.

The newly configured barn contains a billiard room, a home theater and wine cellar on the ground floor, and a main kitchen, dining room, and living room on the main floor. The loft spaces on the upper level look over the original threshing bay of the main barn.

While the owners clearly wished to preserve and celebrate the historic quality of the original barn, they were also open to the reinterpretations of the barn vernacular that this project offered, as evidenced by the corn crib-inspired entry vestibule. Nowhere is this embrace of adaptation more evident than in the reuse of the silo form. Once a common silo, it now houses a circular stair leading to a star-gazing observatory, allowing for full 360-degree views of the night sky.

1   Front elevation
2   Front view

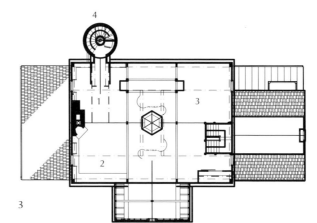

1 Library
2 Study
3 Loft
4 Observatory

3

1 Entry foyer
2 Dining room
3 Living room
4 Piano room
5 Kitchen
6 Main hall
7 Changing room
8 Exercise room
9 Bathroom

4

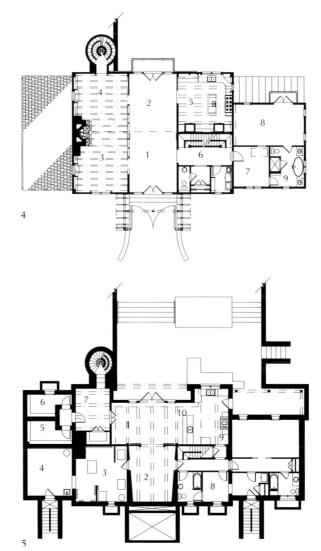

1 Billiard room
2 Theater
3 Mechanical room
4 Workshop
5 Safe
6 Safe
7 Wine room
8 Mud room
9 Recreation room
10 Cabana

5

6

7

3 Loft level plan
4 Upper level plan
5 Ground level plan
6 Rendering
7 Crib entry
8 Pool
9 Paddock view

As with all WESKetch Architecture projects, every effort was made to create a residence that performs with the utmost efficiency. In this case, the high-performance structural insulated panels (SIPS) on the walls and roof, along with radiant heat throughout and top-of-the-line heating and cooling equipment, work together to minimize operating costs and maximize comfort. The resurrection of the Coffeetown Barn represents a unique combination of architecture, preservation, and technology. The end result is a home with historic significance, sumptuous interiors, and comfort beyond compare.

8

9

10

11

12

13

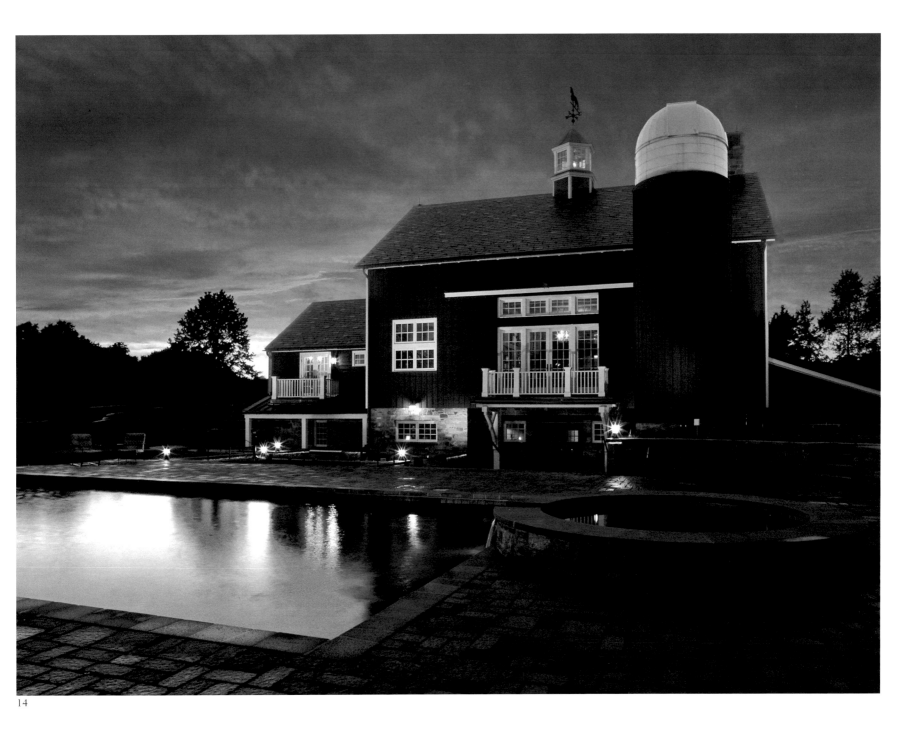

14

10 Wine room
11 Kitchen
12 Barn boards inset in timber frames
13 Living room
14 Swimming pool at rear of house

1

Crosspond Farm

A thorough understanding of site combined with an owner's desire for a traditionally styled American farmhouse resulted in this unique home. Views of lower ponds to the north and natural light approaching from the south created a paradoxical situation that poses light against view. The solution was to provide viewing windows toward the north and allow light to enter the spaces from higher south-facing windows above. The result is a home that maintains a seamless flow with its natural surroundings while maximizing the natural light and views.

The house is imbued with a sense of timelessness through its simple massing and references to the American farmhouse vernacular. Rooms echo with an implied history of place: a bedroom hints at a former life as an upstairs sleeping porch; a sunroom is seemingly created out of a filled-in veranda. These elements combine to bring a character to this home that is rare in new homes of today.

The residence also includes outdoor patios and porches, which frame and highlight the natural beauty surrounding the home.

More impressive than the scope of the design, however, is the eco-friendliness of the residence. The homeowners—avid environmentalists—now enjoy a home constructed with environmentally sensitive materials. The use of certified wood-framing, cedar-roofing, and siding made from concrete are examples of the effort to build both for curb appeal and for a higher purpose.

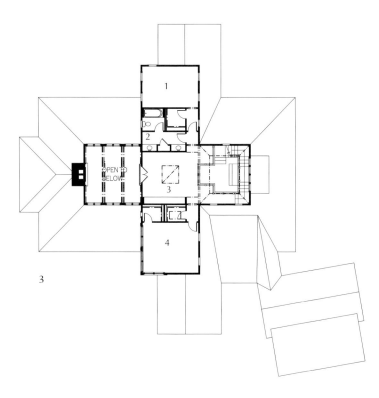

3

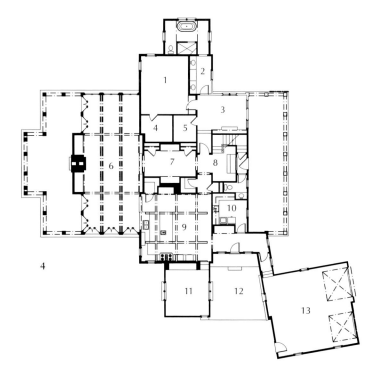

4

5

6

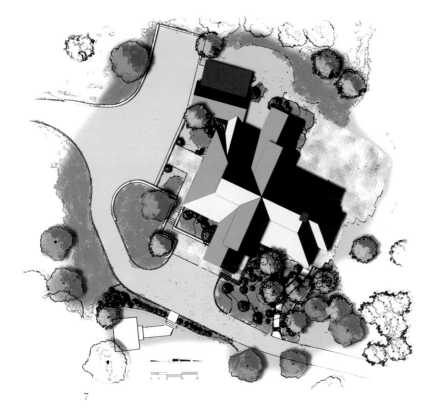

7

8

9

10 Garden terrace
11 Front porch
12 Sunroom overlooking property

10

11

1

Edgewater

Locating a new home in a historic suburb that abuts a lake is an architectural challenge, especially when the home is meant to look as though it has been there forever. However, the owners of this customized home desired a cozy residence that referenced a period English estate or cottage in the country.

The result is a timeless building for the 21st century that also pays close attention to scale, details, and use of materials. The European craftsman elements of this home are rich with detail and are inspired by famous architects such as the distinguished Edwin Lutyens. The brick quoins at the front entry are carefully aligned with the horizontal lines of the façade, while intricately detailed English-style brick is used for the chimneys, and customized brick creates eave detail—all critical elements in expressing the period architecture. In addition, handsome brick piers set the entrance to an open, granite block-lined driveway that flows into a custom mahogany door, framed by a gently curving brick wall.

The success of the project hinged upon the maximum use of a small building envelope, solar orientation, and views of the pond. Brick offered project architects options that other materials could not. Brick also provided a stately presence and does not appear over-scaled for the constrained lot.

2

1 Stair
2 Hall
3 Children's bedroom
4 Closet
5 Bathroom
6 Bathroom
7 Children's bedroom
8 Closet
9 Children's play room
10 Master bedroom
11 Closet
12 Dressing room
13 Master bathroom
14 Closet
15 Hall
16 Office
17 Laundry
18 Bathroom
19 Guest bedroom

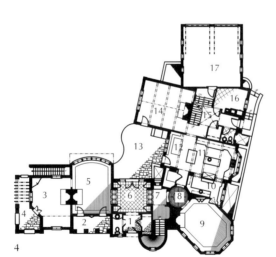

3

1 Entry
2 Veranda
3 Office
4 Office porch
5 Living room
6 Foyer
7 Stair hall
8 Hub
9 Dining room
10 Butlery
11 Kitchen
12 Breakfast area
13 Terrace
14 Family room
15 Mud room
16 Laundry
17 Garage

4

5

6

7

8

9

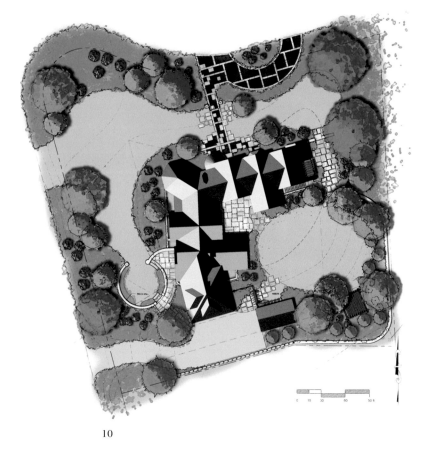

10

11

12

13

Despite being heavily influenced by the English Arts & Crafts movement, the house is overlaid with the most modern, high-performance building techniques of the 21st century. As an environmentally friendly, "green" building material, the hand-made brick is a product that is simultaneously low-maintenance and provides flexibility and durability. This allowed the architects unsurpassed design options and details while offering the homeowners a residence with exceptional energy efficiency, low maintenance, and the durability to last several generations.

As a result, the home has the desired sense of permanence and inviting character requested in the brief. Built in a neighborhood with many historic homes, it is virtually impossible to pick this timeless home from the newly constructed ones because of the finely crafted detail, material choices, and playful exterior elements afforded by the use of brick. Inside, however, the design is state-of-the-art and features all the blessings of the modern era.

14

15 Garden view
16 Front entry
Opposite:
    Sitting garden

15

16

1

Knollwood

Split-level homes are quite a familiar site to the communities of New England. Following the Second World War, many developments were constructed almost entirely of these peculiar multi-floor homes. As the years progressed, the community grew and expanded, yet, forty years later, these homes no longer fit the need of the modern American family.

A split-level offers many problems when trying to renovate or re-create the existing structure. The floor plates are split by a half-flight of stairs, making the flow of circulation through the home difficult to manage. Knollwood is a great example of how a home can be modernized and renovated without removing the existing structure.

The resulting transformation is that of a Shingle Style home, rich in detail. The intersecting Dutch gables are the main focus of the front and offer a hierarchy and a new sense of entry. The front door is pronounced with a gentle, sweeping eyebrow arch and a bowed front stoop.

Outdoor spaces abound with the east porch, while carving out high ceilings from both within the existing home and on the exterior help to open the spaces and interconnect the once-disjointed plan.

2

4

6

1 Future bath
2 Library
3 Bed chamber
4 Sitting room
5 Master foyer
6 Master bath
7 Master closet
8 Closet
9 Kids' loft

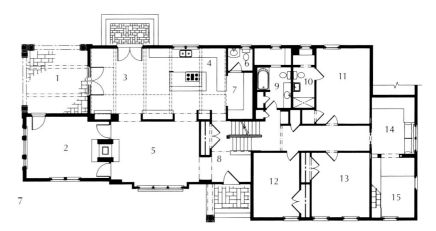

7

1 Porch
2 Music room
3 Breakfast room
4 Kitchen
5 Living room
6 Powder room
7 Pantry
8 Foyer

9 Bathroom
10 Bathroom
11 Bedroom 1
12 Bedroom 2
13 Bedroom 3
14 Kids' study
15 Game room

8　Kitchen from above
9　Kitchen

9

10

11

12

13

10 Front stairs
11 Master bathroom
12 Hall powder room
13 Master bathtub and shower

1

Pineway

This home is a whimsical interpretation of a European-style storybook Tudor home with a central two-story foyer that opens to the dining and living rooms. Through the foyer is a main corridor that acts as the central spine of the home, collecting its occupants and allowing them access to all of the family spaces. The various outdoor spaces, including the raised patios and covered porches, boast a built-in barbecue and a working fire pit.

The exterior is replete with many eye-catching elements such as the conical roof of the stair tower, a large eyebrow dormer, and a handsome chimney. The sumptuous materials give the home a certain tactile quality, expressed in the stone, stucco, and cedar and brick accents.

This is a house that blends harmoniously into the surrounding neighborhood, even with its strong stylistic impressions. The quality of the materials and the refinement of the craftsmanship help to ease the visual originality and link it to a neighborhood of older homes.

2

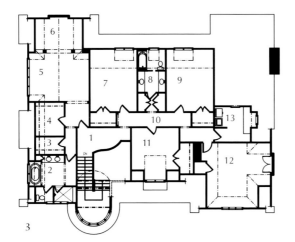

1   Gallery
2   Master bathroom
3   Master closet
4   Second master closet
5   Master bedoom
6   Sitting room
7   Bedoom
8   Bathroom
9   Bedroom
10 Hall
11 Bedroom
12 Office
13 Laundry

3

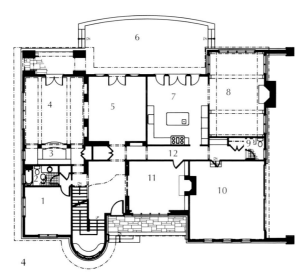

1   Guest bedroom
2   Bathroom
3   Bar
4   Billiard room
5   Living room
6   Terrace
7   Kitchen
8   Family room
9   Powder room
10 Garage
11 Dining room
12 Hall

4

5

6

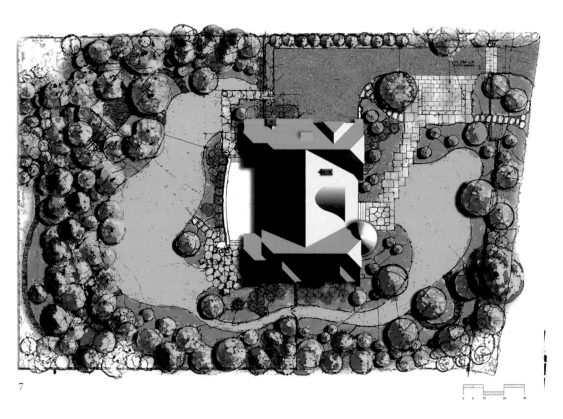

7

8

9

10

11

1

Seagrass

Set along a wide, oceanfront vista, the design of this residence was inspired by the regional, historical homes of the surrounding area. The Shingle Style house is designed to take advantage of the magnificent ocean views and breezes. The front entry with its welcoming milled walls and stair wraps the room as it ascends to the second-floor sleeping quarters.

A cozy study provides for secluded retreats from the activities of a full house. A great room with expansive views to the sea dons a coffered ceiling and a fireplace. The great living room opens to a unique screened porch that is enclosed by the open wraparound porch.

The lower porch, meanwhile, spills into the dunes with a viewing platform, offering a picturesque view of the sea and surrounding landscape while extending the interior of the home outdoors.

1 Front elevation
2 Front of house

2

3

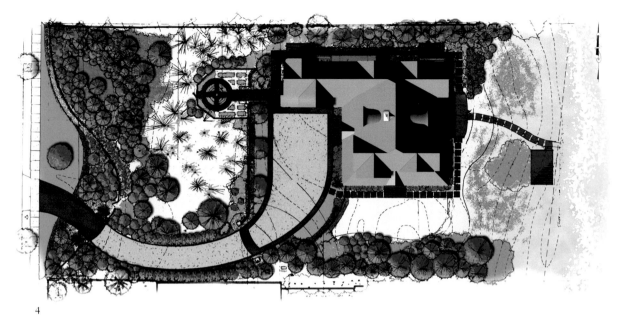

4

5

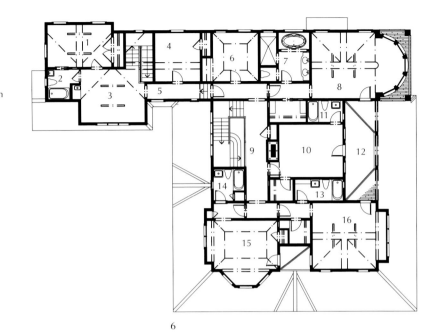

1 Bedroom
2 Bathroom
3 Guest suite sitting room
4 Bedroom
5 Hall
6 Bedroom
7 Master bathroom
8 Master bedroom
9 Hall
10 Bedroom
11 Bathroom
12 Balcony
13 Bathroom
14 Bathroom
15 Bedroom
16 Bedroom

6

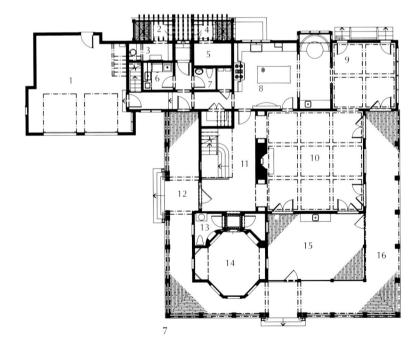

1 Garage
2 Outside shower
3 Dressing room
4 Outside shower
5 Dressing room
6 Laundry
7 Bathroom
8 Kitchen
9 Dining room
10 Living room
11 Foyer
12 Porch
13 Bathroom
14 Guest bedroom
15 Screened-in porch
16 Porch

7

8

10

9

11

12 Living room
13 Kitchen breakfast nook
14 Entry court

12

13

14

1

The Cottage

Around 1900, a chauffeur's cottage complete with a carriage house repair shop was erected to accommodate the day-to-day services of a large estate. The cottage was designed by the renowned architect George Post. When WESKetch Architecture was asked to renovate it more than a century on, the architects found the structure dilapidated and nearly collapsed around its stone foundations.

Now, after a sensitive reconstruction, the entire building, which is less than 2000 square feet, is nestled at a woodland edge, along with a small farm shed and pump house. Inside, the first-floor workshop has been replaced with a living space and kitchen, complete with stone fireplace, while a south patio covered by a cedar trellis has been constructed from logs cut from the site.

The cottage was remodeled with a sensitive fusion of the latest building technology and the kind of hand-crafted quality that was used hundreds of years ago. Highlights throughout the home include the solid cedar beams and truss work; fieldstone veneer stone walls with 1-foot-thick framing to authenticate the effect of a solid stone wall; a hand-split cedar shake roof; and reclaimed hand-cut cedar logs. Antique chimney pots were also imported from England to cap the chimneys. Antique doors, meanwhile, have been modified and reclaimed, while solid rusticated barn beams have been put to good use in the interior. Operable hand-made wooden window and door shutters and complementary flower boxes help blend the building into the natural surroundings.

1   Front elevation
2   Side view
3   Rear view
4   Front view

2

3

4

5

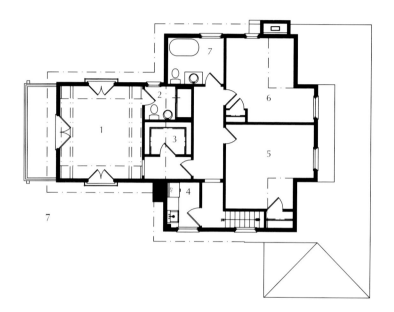

1 Master bedroom
2 Master bath
3 Master closet
4 Laundry
5 Bedroom
6 Bedroom
7 Bathroom

7

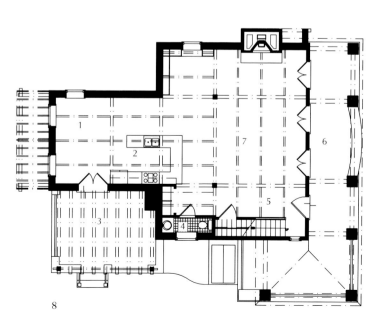

1 Breakfast room
2 Kitchen
3 Pergola
4 Powder room
5 Entry
6 Porch
7 Living room

6

8

1

Windsong

So many restoration projects begin with a familiar phrase: "this place has potential" or "that old house must have been something in its day." This home was a modest Victorian with character and presence, but years of the shore's salty winds and intense sun had taken their toll. A sensitive addition and carefully detailed renovation have successfully breathed new life to this bayside home, while fulfilling the promise of its potential and revitalizing its historic charm.

One enters the home through a double cascading staircase that perfectly accentuates the coastal feel of this Victorian, situated in Barnegat Bay. The residence, originally constructed at the turn of the 19th century, underwent a renovation and addition that not only kept the home's historic charm intact, but also added new components that seamlessly blend with the historical elements of the residence. More then a century on, however, these now-outdated renovations had been complicated by the decline and decaying nature of the house. Floorboards were sinking and the bathrooms were in complete disrepair. Windows were drooping and previous modifications to the home had now become unsightly and unnecessary.

2

3

4

With the help of historic photographs, WESKetch Architecture set about restoring the pristine charm. Flying trusses at the end of the gabled roof, combined with blusters, spindles, and porch railings, lend an authentic Victorian feel to the outside of the home. Inside, the living spaces were smartly renovated to handle extended family visits.

The old bathrooms were removed and three new bathrooms were stacked in a dominating tower feature.

The combination of renovations to the existing residence and new additions that respect the character and history of the original have been successfully merged into a home that can be enjoyed by multiple generations of family at once. With these sensitive updates, it will continue to provide a seaside haven for generations to come.

5

6

7

8

9

1

Wingspan

As a result of the post-Second World War building boom, the suburban landscape is now littered with mass building byproducts of the 1950s. Wingspan is one solution to the ranch style of that era. As in all whole-house renovations, this home stems from the original form and intent of the existing building, coupled with the owner's vision and functional needs. The need for integration of scale and form is an essential ingredient to a harmonious neighborhood.

The crafted, Shingle Style form is a transformation well-received by the ranch. The roof pitches can be modestly manipulated to achieve multi-story living while keeping within a contextual scale of the surrounding community. Detailed façades make for the merging of craftsmanship with form, and natural cedar shingles breathe life and texture into any building.

This particular renovation called for a dramatic transformation of the entire house, beginning with the garden/pool side and finishing with the front. As is the case in most renovations, the need to phase projects may be a necessity for both spatial and economic needs. If the home was torn down, the project might have been stripped of its detailed dignity, not to mention the fact that its occupants would have had to seek shelter

2

3

4

elsewhere during the construction process. As it happens, the design solution allowed for the renovation of the rear of the residence, including the kitchen, breakfast room, family room, guest suite, and dining room expansion on the first floor, and the master suite on the second floor, to be completed the first year. The front entry foyer, library, stair-hall, and children's bedrooms were completed the next year.

The rear of the residence has a dynamic playful form that encourages informal entertaining and activity and is garnished with garden-like elements such as trellises, columns, patios, and porches. The front façade secures the formal presence of the structure with symmetrical roof lines.

3 Street view
4 Pergola
5 Clerestory window detail

5

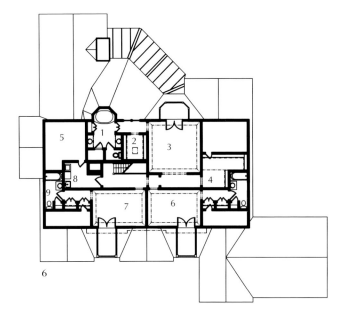

1 Master bathroom
2 Walk-in closet
3 Master bedroom
4 Walk-in closet
5 Bathroom
6 Bedroom
7 Bedroom
8 Laundry
9 Bathroom

6

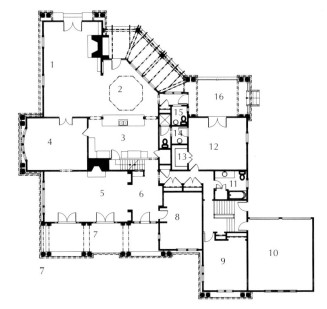

1 Family room
2 Breakfast area
3 Kitchen
4 Dining room
5 Living room
6 Foyer
7 Porch
8 Library
9 Guest bedroom
10 Garage
11 Bathroom
12 Bedroom
13 Closet
14 Bathroom
15 Powder room
16 Covered patio

7

8

9

6 Upper level plan
7 Ground level plan
8 Window detail
9 Porch

10 Column detail
11 Balcony
12 Pool

10

11

Awards, Accolades, and Publications

Awards and Accolades

Ranked 12th in the Nation for "Best Architectural Firm to Work For" by Zweig/White, September 2007
Recipient of "Forty Under 40" Award from NJ Biz, November 2006
Brick in Home Building Awards, Best in Class–Custom Design for Edgewater, October 2006
Ranked 15th in the Nation for "Best Architectural Firm to Work For" by Zweig/White, September 2006
Ludwici Roof Tile Crown Award, Summer 2003
Palladio Awards, *Period Homes* magazine: Sympathetic Addition Winner, June 2002
American Institute of Architects – NJ: Young Architect of the Year, 2001
New Jersey CANstruction: Structural Ingenuity Award, Fall 2001
Custom Home magazine: Design Award, 2001
Awarded LEED accreditation by United States Green Building Council (first architect in New Jersey to receive this accreditation), January 2000
Architects, Designers, Planners for Social New York: Responsibility Award
International Design Competition: "Childhood in the City", First Place
American Concrete Structures Association: Pre-cast Design Competition, First Place
New Jersey School of Architecture: Excellence in Design Award, Fall 1988
Many Nagle Award, Spring 1990

Publications
Periodicals

"Coffee Town Barn," *Architectural Digest*, 2008 feature article
"Palomaki Home is a Convenient Truth," by Janet Erwood, *Relevant Times*, Jan/Feb 2008
"Turn up the Heat," by Meg Fox, Robin Amster, and Ren Miller, *Design NJ*, Feb/Mar 2008
"Eco Design," *NJ Life*, April 2007, p. 46
"Cross Pond Farms," by Donna Boyle Schwartz, *New York Spaces*, June/July 2006, pp. 82–85
"Victorian at Sea," by Iyna Bort Caruso, *Design NJ*, December 2005/January 2006, pp. 154–161
"A Nod to the Past," by D.M. Catherine, *Design NJ*, June/July 2005, pp. 140–5.

"Edgewater"; *Brick in Architecture: The 2004 Residential Issue*, Vol 61, No 4, pp. 5–7.
"Look Before You Leap: How to Choose the Right Architect for Your Project," by William E.S. Kaufman,
    Casa Design for Living, May 2004, pp. 50–52, 58
"Digital Architect," by Deborah Snoonian P.E., *Architectural Record*, September 2003, p. 187
"The Lighted Path of Evolution," by William E.S. Kaufman (contributing writer), *Casa Design for Living*,
    November/December 2003, pp. 55–58
"Functional Kidspaces," by William E.S. Kaufman (contributing writer), *Casa Design for Living*,
    September/October 2003, pp. 12–13
"Architecture: Designing for Life in the 21st Century," by William E. S. Kaufman (contributing
writer), *Casa Design for Living*, September/October 2003; pp. 18–20
"Traditional Green," by William E.S. Kaufman (contributing writer), *Casa Design for Living*, March/April 2003,
    pp. 10–12
"The Emerald Palace," by Johanna R. Ginsberg, *NJIT Magazine*, Fall 2002/Winter 2003, pp. 17–20
"Traditionally Green," by William E.S. Kaufman, *Traditional Building Magazine*, October 2002, pp. 46–49
"Exterior Excitement," *Design NJ*, Fall 2002; pp. 116–117
"Structurally Sound: Ideas for enhancing the garden with arbors, gazebos and more," *Design NJ*,
    August/September 2002, pp. 69–71
"A Towering Addition," *Period Homes*, Summer 2002, pp. 10–11
"The Estates of New Jersey," Recorder Community Newspaper, August 11, 2001
"Under the Eaves," *Custom Home*, July/August 2001, pp. 66–68
"Asphalt-y Reasoning," Letter to the Editor, *This Old House*, March 2000, p. 16
"Great Renovations: Rooms With a View," *NJ Monthly*, March 2000, p. 57
"Picture This: Virtual software design programs make house plans spring into three dimensional life,"
    This Old House, Jan/Feb 2000, p. 51
"Demolition Derby," *NJ Monthly*, May 1999, pp. 58–61, 79, 98
"The Road Home, Driveways deserve more than just paving," *This Old House*, April 1999, pp. 40, 42
"Saving the Ranch," *This Old House*, March 1999, pp. 40–42, 44, 46

Newspapers and electronic media
The New York Times, 19 November 2003, "WESKetch puts a new spin on 1906 silk factory,"
    by Antoinette Martin
Echoes-Sentinel, November 2001, "Building a Firm to be Proud of"
Bernardsville News, January, 1999, "Save Mine Brook Road"
Courier News, 1998, "Save Mine Brook Road"
"Men in Tool Belts," PBS Television Show, 1998
Newark Star Ledger, September, 1998

Books
Dream Homes of New Jersey, Panache Publishing, pp. 114–119, May 2007
The New 100 Houses x 100 Architects, "Windsong," The Images Publishing Group, Melbourne, Australia,
    2007, pp. 332–335
A Pocketful of Houses, The Images Publishing Group, Melbourne, Australia, 2006
The Somerset Hills: Volume I, "Appletrees," Mountain Colony Press, Far Hills, NJ, 2004, pp. 29– 31
Updating Classic American Capes, by Jane Gitlin, "Trial Size to Family Size," Taunton Press, Newtown, CT,
    2003, pp. 124–131
Another 100 of the World's Best Houses, "Edgewater," The Images Publishing Group, Melbourne, Australia,
    2003, pp. 74–78
1000 Architects, The Images Publishing Group, Melbourne, Australia, 2003, p. 562

Project Credits

Appletrees, Bernardsville, New Jersey
Contractor:	Duffy Construction
Interior Designer:	Owner
Photographs:	Jay Rosenblatt and David Groul

Beechwood, New Vernon, New Jersey
Contractor:	Grecco Construction
Landscape Designer:	Back to Nature
Interior Designer:	Frank Delle Donne Interiors Inc.
Photographs:	Rob Kern and Jay Rosenblatt

Bridle Paths, Bernardsville, New Jersey
Contractor:	Grecco Construction
Landscape Designer:	Back to Nature
Interior Designer:	Jeffrey Haines, Butters Far Hills
Photographs:	David Groul

Clarence Manor, Montville, New Jersey
Contractor:	JW Custom Homes
Landscape Designer:	Tapestry Landscape Architects + Scenic Landscape
Interior Designer:	Cynthia Harriman of Eastern Designs
Photographs:	Jay Rosenblatt

Coffeetown Barn, Bedminster, New Jersey
Contractor:	Solid Wood Construction
Barn:	NJ Barn Company
Landscape Designer:	Conceptual Landscapes
Interior Designer:	Owner
Photographs:	Jay Rosenblatt

Crosspond Farm, Basking Ridge, New Jersey
    Contractor: Alto Enterprises
    Landscape Designer: Back to Nature
    Interior Designer: Charles O. Schwarz
    Photographs: Rob Kern

Edgewater, Short Hills, New Jersey
    Contractor: Grecco Construction
    Landscape Designer: Back to Nature
    Interior Designer: Lars Spicer
    Photographs: Jay Rosenblatt

Knollwood, Short Hills, New Jersey
    Contractor: Norcon Development
    Interior Designer: bhome – Tracy Butler
    Photographs: Jay Rosenblatt

Pineway, New Providence, New Jersey
    Contractor: Duffy Construction
    Landscape Designer: Back to Nature Landscape Associates
    Interior Designer: WESK Interiors, Inc.
    Photographs: Rob Kern & Jay Rosenblatt

Seagrass, Mantoloking, New Jersey
    Contractor: Alto Enterprises
    Landscape Designer: Chris DePhillips Landscape Design
    Interior Architecture: WESK Architecture
    Photographs: Jay Rosenblatt

The Cottage, Bernardsville, New Jersey
    Contractor: Duffy Construction
    Interior Designer: Owner
    Photographs: David Groul

Windsong, Seaside Park, New Jersey
    Landscape Designer: Cross River Design
    Interior Designer: WESK Interiors, Inc.
    Photographs: Bruce Nelson

Wingspan, Short Hills, New Jersey
    Contractor: MIKA, Lou Mandarakis
    Landscape Designer: ELA
    Interior Designer: Frank Della Donne
    Photographs: Jay Rosenblatt

Firm biography

WESKetch Architecture, Inc. was founded in 1993 with a vision to blend timeless traditional design with the best of modern innovation. Experiencing quick and unprecedented growth, principal and founder William E.S. Kaufman assembled a team that soon gained a national reputation for outstanding work. Today, WESKetch is recognized throughout the country for being a leader in sustainable initiatives and award-winning design.

At the forefront of innovation, Kaufman was the first LEED (Leadership in Energy and Environmental Design) accredited professional architect in New Jersey. As the father of three children, he recognized the imminent need for safer, healthier buildings to work and live in. As such, the firm has embraced this mentality and is celebrated for creating healthy environments while maintaining impeccable aesthetics.

Beyond the scope of architecture, WESKetch is also involved with interior design and construction management. This holistic approach to design streamlines the building process by improving communication and providing seamless process from design through construction. As part of this framework, the firm feels that a truly superior structure is one that is integrated with the site.

Perhaps due to this unique framework, it is no surprise that the firm has been featured prominently in popular magazines such as *Architectural Digest, New York Spaces, This Old House Magazine, Traditional Building, Design NJ*, and *Architectural Record* among others. Notably, *Custom Home* Magazine honored WESKetch with a Merit Award for outstanding work in the field. Further proof of this ingenuity and passion for excellence has resulted in recognition at the local level. Prominent among these include extensive features in the *Newark Star-Ledger* and *New Jersey Monthly* magazine.

Mr. Kaufman has seen his fair share of attention over the past few years. In 2001, he was named the American Institute of Architecture's Young Architect of the Year for the state of New Jersey. NJ Biz tabbed him as one of their Forty Under 40 for 2006. He is frequently asked to write opinion-editorial pieces for both trade and mainstream media outlets. Kaufman first made a splash in the media in 2003 when he co-hosted *Casa Bella*, a local programming show that featured design and building trends. In 2007, he appeared on the popular show *One on One with Steve Adubato* that appeared in markets including Boston, New York, Philadelphia, and Baltimore, where he discussed his design philosophy and "green" architecture. In addition, the firm has twice been profiled on NBC's magazine-style show *Open House New York* that airs on the network's affiliate station in the tri-state area.

The secret to the firm's success remains simple. It lies in the instilled belief in the studio process—the idea of allowing each design professional within the firm to contribute in his or her unique way to every project. Weekly design critiques allow the power of collaborative thinking to raise the proverbial bar of creativity beyond that of a single source. From the minds of many comes the brilliance that is now associated with each and every project.